Can't Die Mom

Peggy Nolan

DEDICATION

To my daughters Jessica and Christina
and
to my forever husband, Richard

ACKNOWLEDGMENTS

Special thanks to my writing mentors, Laurie Wagner and Marc Olmsted.

PRAISE FOR CAN'T DIE MOM

"I've always believed that when women share their truth from a place of vulnerability and authenticity their words have the power to transform lives. In **Can't Die Mom!***, breast cancer survivor Peggy Nolan courageously does just that as she opens her heart and journal to share some of the rawest and most painful moments of her life."* ~ **Linda Joy, Publisher** ~ Aspire Magazine www.Aspire10Years.com and Best-selling Publisher at www.InspiredLivingPublishing.com

***

"When we share our truth from a deep and tender place, we break open and heal. Raw, vulnerable and courageously speaking from her heart and soul, Peggy Nolan reveals her truth so we can see our own light in the dark. Through her powerful poems, she gives us a glimpse of how to lovingly transform our lives." ~ **Dr. Debra Reble,** International Best-selling Author, Psychologist, and Love Ambassador at www.debrareble.com

***

"Is it possible to live a whole life – all of its heartache and joy – in 29 pages? If you're Peggy Nolan, it most certainly is. In this slim, raw and superb volume of poetry, Nolan winds the reader through a personal journey of love, betrayal, death and renewal that is startling in its frank depiction of a life well and sometimes painfully lived. Nolan uses the lens of poetry – simple, direct words and short, but powerful lines – to encompass some of life's greatest challenges; breast cancer, a lover's betrayal, the ache of war. And yet, somehow, this collection will leave you inspired and uplifted. The most startling take-away from **Can't Die Mom***? Take a moment to breathe."* ~ **Dan Szczesny,** Travel Writer and Journalist at www.danszczesny.com

CONTENTS

A FEW WORDS ABOUT WAR

Holding the hands
of my two little girls
I stand on the tarmac
with 3,000 other people

Watching the distant light
in the dark March sky
grow bigger and brighter

as the United Airline's 747
crawls its way towards
Myrtle Beach Air Force Base

A deep voice over the PA
announces, "plane's on approach
it's twenty miles out."

A cheer ripples through the crowd
family members, townspeople, the media
welcoming home 400 members of the
357th Tactical Fighter Wing

America's Gulf War veterans
One of them – my husband
A man I haven't seen in 210 days

As the plane's headlight grows bigger
- I remember -

Iraq's invasion of Kuwait
Bush's mad dash to create
a coalition of nations

Stormin' Norman and the 101st Airborne
Apache helicopters breaking down
in the sands of Arabia

The Army's request
for the Wart Hog...the Tank Killer...the Flying Gaitlin Gun...
the A-10 Thunderbolt

In late August before Jessica turned six
War came to Myrtle Beach
She learned new words

Operation Desert Shield
Chemical warfare, mobility bag, gas mask,
Republican Guard, Saddam Hussein
Why does Daddy have to go so far away?

Under house arrest
chained down by the phone
we knew would ring
It's time to go

Trying not to cry
He kissed his girls goodbye
Scared he'd never see them again

I drove him to the airfield
Silence serenaded by the gentle hum
of the Subaru's engine

We made love the night before
We said all we could say

We're making the world safe for crude oil
and rescuing a country that
didn't exist before World War II

I parked the car

his blue eyes bloodshot and puffy
I gave him one last kiss goodbye

Dressed in camouflage battle dress uniform
his mobility bag in hand
I watched my husband as he made
the slow walk to the waiting C-5

A woman I didn't know
handed me a plastic yellow bow
made from a large Hefty garbage bag
"You need this more than I do" she said.

Too numb to thank her
I drove back home
and called my landlord
I wanted dead bolts on all the doors

Alone in my house
the waiting over
relieved he was gone
missing him already

One last call from Spain
then nothing for weeks until
the mail service caught up

I remember the letters
the life line that kept us connected
He wrote every day – sometimes eight times a day
I won the competition for most letters in one delivery – 32

We played a game, my husband and I
One word per envelope
No postage necessary

While he waited in the desert
Jessica turned six

Christina turned three
and I turned twenty seven

He missed Thanksgiving and Christmas
and he told his father to send me
a dozen long stemmed roses for
our seventh anniversary

While he ducked from wayward scuds
I went to college
raised our girls
and while cleaning out the attic
I fell through the floor

on my right side bruised and bleeding
from my wrist to my waist
I hung from a 2×4 until Jessica
heard my banshee scream

While he filled sandbags
I moved from off-base to on-base housing
I mowed the lawn and
entertained his mother on December 25th

One morning mid January
the conflict on the brink
He called to tell me
the F-16's stopped for gas

At 6:50PM that same day
I watch Peter Jennings on TV
he's pre-empted by the war

Bernard Shaw and whatshisface
trapped in a Baghdad hotel
filming aack-aack
as it lit up the pre-dawn sky

My phone began to ring
the military wives' recall roster
We all check in

"It's started."
"You Okay?"
"Yup"
"Gotta go." Click

I called my dad
the only time I cried
"war's not supposed to happen to us."

Tears interrupted when Jessica shrieks
A gaping hole where her first loose tooth
used to be

Biting down on the end of a towel
She had Christina yank the other end
There's blood all over the kitchen floor
oddly comic – it's a Kodak moment

F-16's dropping precision bombs
Battleships launching cruise missiles
Bernard Shaw is hiding underneath his
hotel room bed

Operation Desert Storm
A three week air slaughter
a four day ground romp
Iraqi troops surrender to CNN

The Iraqi Army obliterated
The Kingdom of Kuwait restored
The ghosts of Viet Nam vanquished
No one I know died

For the duration is over

at 7:30 AM
I got the call
"he's on the plane."

Due to arrive at 10 PM
I went to school
Got an A on my French test
and talked my way out of
a speeding ticket

The plane's in full view
I watch it land and taxi
to the spot reserved for
distinguished visitors

The crowd presses forward
afraid to lose my girls
I death grip their little hands

The doors to the plane swing open
the first desert rat steps out and waves
Jumping up and down, Christina and Jessica yell
D A D D Y

We swarm the plane as
the returning heroes disembark
I search the crowd for my husband
they all look the same
in chocolate chip uniforms

A stranger hoists Christina on her shoulders
from her higher vantage point
she spots him first and squeals
with the same delight
as having ice cream for breakfast

My husband and I
gaze hungrily upon each other

as he hugs both our daughters
he captures me with his smile and mouths
 "I love you."

DIVORCE IN THREE PARTS

Kill Me Please (Part I)

Can't eat cardboard tasting oatmeal
Can't sleep adrenaline flooding blood vessels
Can't function body on autopilot

breath labors shallow
saggy bloodshot eyes

Boa constrictor

crushing my bones

After nineteen years

Why did he leave?

Don't Piss Me Off (Part II)

He called today
Screaming at me

Because I hired a lawyer

Because I won't file
A joint tax return

Because I won't give him
Fifteen hundred dollars

Signed, Sealed, Delivered (NOT Yours) – Part III

July 22 – graduation day
I received my divorce diploma
through the United States Postal Service

A do-over midway
starting at forty

CAN'T DIE MOM

I've worked the exercise
Write your own eulogy
Who's at your funeral

One day I got bad news
Invasive breast cancer
the only thought running through my mind
"I can die from this."

I got drunk at lunch
sobered up at work
called my parents - went home

Spent the evening with my daughters
They were scared - I could tell
The three of us, curled up on my bed
Watching a romance movie Under the Tuscan Sun

After the movie, they went to bed
I lay in mine, crying as quietly as I could

Crazy - the only thing that I could think of
Get your affairs in order
Make sure Darren has no claim to your assets
Those belong to Jessica and Christina

Thinking of Christina
Made me cry even harder
I'm not finished with her

I tossed in bed
Do I bother Jessica? Do I cry in front of her?
What the hell - I got up and went to her room

laid down next to her

She wrapped her arms around me
My head in her lap
Her eyes tired and red
"I don't know what to say," she said.

"just let me cry."
"you can't die mom" her voice stoic
"I know - " I trailed off

II.

What scared me most -

Dying before Christina turned 18

before Jessica graduated from
college

before Christina finished high school

Dying before shopping for wedding dresses

before seeing my daughters walk
down the aisle

before meeting my grand-babies

Dying without knowing what it feels like
to have a man truly madly deeply in love with me

Dying before seeing the Grand Canyon

spending a month or two island
hopping through Greece

before hiking the Scottish Highlands in
July

before seeing the Aurora Borealis in Alaska

Dying before making a difference

III.

A funny thing happened on the way to the notary

I needed a witness watch
me sign my life away

at that moment
I was ready to die

this
amazing calm

now I don't wear a watch

I stopped looking for that special someone
I took up golf
I went indoor rock climbing

I started my own business
I didn't die when I got laid off
I travel here and there when I want to
...I just do it...

Death will eventually catch up with me
Until then

I don't ask permission

NO SHAVING REQUIRED

Clear liquid infused through an IV
A bald head

Drip
 drip

Tired beyond tired
Joints ache; head hurts

Drip
 drip

Adryomicin, Cytoxin, Taxol
Zofram, Compazine, Decadron

Drip
 drip

No shaving required

THE SCAR

How many times
Have I looked at this scar
The scar that reminds me
"You had cancer"

How many times
Have I looked at this scar
and mourned the loss
of my precious left breast

How many times
Have I looked at this scar
and felt the uneven healing skin
stitching herself together

How many times
Have I looked at this scar
and heard the words
"We caught it early,"
"We can treat this,"
"You'll be just fine"

How many times
Have I looked at this scar
and wondered
"Will I ever be sexy,"
"Will I ever be desirable"

How many times
Have I looked at this scar
and noticed the intricate work
of a skilled breast surgeon

How many times
Have I looked at this scar
and gave thanks to be in the artistic hands
of the best plastic surgeon in Boston

How many times
Have I looked at this scar
and rejoiced in the love
so effortlessly given to me

How many times
Have I looked at this scar
and applauded my posse
for the strength and courage they mustered
to see me through

How many times
Have I looked at this scar
only to smile
because I'm here today
and very alive

DREAMING MY FUTURE

An outside wedding
Sherbet orange wispy clouds
In my dream - A setting sun
Tuxedos and glittering evening gowns
Sitting in chairs lined with white bows
On freshly cut grass

I'm dressed in a gray pin-striped suit
More ready for a meeting with the CEO
Why am I here?
Out of place; out of time

A faceless man appears
He leads me to a plywood stage
"You're the entertainment" he says

He seats me at a drab metal desk
The kind no longer found in office space
A microphone, like the one Johnny Carson used, stares at me

The faceless man presses a card into my hand
"You can only talk about what's printed here…
and you have to be funny," he whispered in my ear

In bold black letters

O-R-A-N-G-E
Perplexed and Confused
I looked at the faceless man
"I'm supposed to be funny about orange?"

He never answered; he just walked away.
I looked at the card
I looked at the sky
A deepening blood orange sky
I searched the crowd of wedding guests
Did I know anyone here?
A woman dressed in white
She must be the bride
She caught my gaze and smiled a waiting smile

I looked at the card again
Something funny about Orange
A sound gurgled up from my stomach
I tried to stifle it

Hand over mouth
And I snorted
Which made me laugh
And I couldn't stop
The microphone amplified
uncontrollable infectious laughter

Tears rolled down my face

This soulful laughter
This cleansing laughter
This contagious laughter
And all around me
The sound of laughter;
the color orange

JAMES SPADER, TOO

Hotel room at the Sheraton
St. Louis, Missouri
I stayed here once

Paisley covered bed spread...matching curtains...in bed I straddle
James Spader underneath me...wearing a black business
suit...talking on his cell phone...I lean over and whisper in his ear,
"Take me on a date."

Pursing chicken beak lips, "I'm out of work...contract's canceled."
His steely gray eyes stare me down.

Sitting up, I tilt my head, "But I just saw you and Captain Kirk last
night," the pitch of my voice slightly higher.

He flips his cell phone shut and quietly grumbles,
"That show shot 6 months ago...show's canceled."

face a question mark
thinking he's joking
Boston Legal canceled?

Voices in the hallway...I vault from the bed...jerk open hotel room
door...Poke my head out...it's my gray-haired step mother...and
some woman who looks vaguely familiar...She knows me...she's
smiling and shrieking my
name...maybe it's Anne with short hair

I start to sweat...nauseous panic choking me...
shut the door...double bolt it...hide James Spader

Out the window I follow...Bare feet on cobblestone...he's leaning
up against a lamp post...Talking on his cell phone again...I wrap
my arms around his neck...A close
up shot...My lips to his ear, "I loved you in Stargate."

James Spader fades away
Scotty beamed him up
I'm not outside

Standing in the middle of the paisley covered hotel room
A bell boy at the door...crimson red pants...starched white jacket

Three black suitcases
someone's checked in
I haven't checked out

THE BUS RIDE

Sitting next to me
He smiles 'good morning'
A splash of Burberry
A puff of Marlboro
A hint of Arabica
Breathing in his scent
A slow burn
Adrenaline unleashed
Racing through veins
Mario Andretti at the wheel
Knees touch
Skin prickles
On high alert
Heat rising
Cheeks red
Uncomfortably intoxicating

DRIVING HOME

Following red tail lights
Passing white steeple church
Remembering the taste
of his wine soaked lips

APPROACHING ALBUQUERQUE

Looking out
the airplane window
Eight new shades of brown

JESSICA AT 3

Canary yellow mini-skirt
Grabbing her plastic pink purse
She struts the morning dew

WHAT'S FOR DINNER?

Moldy salad
Fermented apple juice
Rancid watermelon -
Frozen raviolis again

BEST FRIENDS

high heel shoe fetish
addicted to lipstick
Together, 12 years old again

SIGN

Driving behind
construction truck
Yellow sign - "Do Not Follow"

8AM

Underneath the covers
Curled in C
Naked bodies wake
If only for a moment
We share one breath
and watch morning rise

THE PIER

One block away
from Hotel Carmel

Hotdogs and crowds
Bubba Gump's and movie trivia
Amusement park rides and four tickets a piece

The sound of the Pacific Ocean
crashing into wooden pylons

Pigeons flying overhead
Bird shit in my hair

THE PROBLEM WITH FLINTSTONES

"Look Mommy," She proclaimed.
"I ate all my snack!"

Her three year old hands
held up the empty bottle
of Flintstones vitamins
with iron

A child-proof bottle
100 count
gone
eaten
Mistaken for a snack

I picked up the phone
dialed poison control

Do not pass go
Do not collect $200
Go directly to the emergency room

Ipecac to vomit
charcoal to absorb
lethal levels of iron

I never bought
vitamins again

OUTSIDE THE WIRE

got the call
It's time to pack
kevlar and gear
off to Iraq

combat landing zone
C130 spiraling down
The Iraqi desert
six shades of brown

rolling stop
disembark
Overhead a rocket pops

The Big Snake, Balad Air Base
Camp Anaconda, Mortaritaville
Different names; same place

Convoy missions
must stay awake
in the dead of night
for strawberry cheesecake

Outside the wire
under live fire

arrive alive
steak tips for chow

LIFE GOES ON

Overheard conversation
in the oncology waiting room

"How bad is it?' she asked.

"Stage IV," I heard the reply.

The lady with the gray hair
tilted her head
nodded and sighed
lips pressed together...
Perhaps not sure what to say.

"Why don't you come over Friday night," said the one with Stage
IV. "We just bought a new hot tub."

MANDY

I.

All she ever wanted
was to be a mom

Four beautiful children
liver disease
a life cut short

cirrhosis
the doctors said
she never drank

oxygen helped her breathe
equipment monitored
heart rate and blood pressure
the nurse's call button within reach

the hum of life sustaining machines
the occasional beeping sound
alerting the nurse on duty
to check-in

I stood by her bedside
holding her hand
stroking her hair

"Hey beautiful," I said

"I'm not the pretty one,"
she struggled to say.
"You are."

I shook my head
tried to smile

wiped away
tears instead

My brother stood
at the foot of her bed
rubbing her feet

"I'm cold" she said
to no one in particular

"Think of some place warm,"
my brother replied.

Light sparkled and danced
inside her dark brown eyes

"Did you know," she whispered
"I'm taking Meg back to Panama
when she turns 18."

"How fun!" this time I smiled.

She squeezed my hand
and gazed at me with ferocious intensity
"Will you go?"

II.

Crowded into the
sterile hospital room
dressed in yellow paper gowns
we stood twenty strong

Holding hands
passing tissues
sharing memories
sometimes laughing
sometimes crying

wiping tears
blowing noses

surrounded by
her circle of love
life support shut off
she took her last breath

WHAT I'VE BEEN TAUGHT

Be quiet
Be seen and not heard.

Ladies don't finish the last bite
and you'll get fat if you eat that.

Don't ask questions,
Raise your hand if you want to be called on.

Never show the world you're angry
and don't shine too brightly.

You're not that good at math
you're not that good at this or that either

You're cute but not pretty.

You're a peacemaker, a know-it-all, and kind of bossy.

Keep smiling
suck it up
you're grounded.

At 40 I unlearned everything I'd been taught.

SERENDIPITY SLIDING SIDEWAYS

Weeding through my junk mail
Minding my own business
An email from my first boyfriend

Someone I haven't seen
in 25 years
A blast from the past
oh Wow!

I had to pay
Fifteen dollars
just to read his email
on Classmates.com

I emailed him back
and gave him
both my numbers

Sure!
I'd love to see you again
and catch up
on all those years

He calls me the next day
I see his name
in my caller ID

I let the phone ring
three times
before I answer it

I can barely speak
Hello?
The sound of his voice
it's the same

I hear him
what is he saying?

I look at the clock
we've been talking
for 15 minutes

it seems like yesterday
we were making out
in the hallway
near the lockers
before my first class

I have to cut him short
I have to go to a meeting
Damn!

So I asked him
"are you busy tonight?
can you meet for coffee?"

He says he's free
and that he love to see me

It's 9PM
as I pull into the
Denny's parking lot

I'm a little late
he's a little early

I walk in
And see him sitting there
In a booth
Facing the front door
So he can see me
I hope I look good
I hope I'm not too fat

I can't believe
it's him

He stands up
And we hug hello
This incredible hug
I let go
But he's still holding me
And I know
Right then and there
I know
I will buy that car when I see it
And I see it

I'm sitting across from
the man
who once was
the boy
I first fell in love with

This sense of WOW
Flips me
up
side
down

WHEN REST CALLS

I want to rest
Rest into deep meaningful books and books of pure fantasy.

I want to rest
Feeling the texture of yarn as it slips through my fingers as I
complete the next stitch; the next row.

I want to rest
Deeply into the act of creating no longer feeling this constant
pressing forward, this need to achieve.

I want to rest
Joyfully into the giggles of my grandchildren, to experience the
wonder and awe of this world through the eyes of a six year old.

I want to rest
and taste the meaning of life with each delightful bite, never mind
the scale or the few extra pounds.

I want to rest in the arms of the man I love somewhere on a beach
watching the sunset knowing there is nothing to achieve and no
place else I'd rather be.

Yes. I want to rest. To sit right here and Breathe.

LOVE IS A CHOICE

(This story first appeared in the bestselling Kindle book, "The Wisdom of Midlife Women 2")

Christopher met me in the hospital hallway and gave me a ginormous hug. He had just become a father and the nurses were allowing one family member in the recovery room at a time. After his mom and his girlfriend mom, I was the next person Christopher asked for.

"Well, Dad," I drew out the word *dad*. Perhaps to make it real for me. My stepson...a dad!

He looked at me with his lopsided grin. Christopher's hair was a mess and I could tell he hadn't slept much.

"I bet you never thought you'd see this day," he half-joked.

"I always knew I'd see this day." I smiled at him as I choked back a few tears.

Nine years earlier, I met Christopher just after he turned 14. He was on the small side and he looked and acted closer to 10 than to being a teenager. When my husband, Richard, and I got married, he gifted me with four children to add to the two I had from my first marriage. Christopher was his youngest and the only one still living at home. He came with a few challenges - he was socially delayed, learning delayed, obsessive compulsive, and he put the H in ADHD.

Despite his *isms*, I naively thought life as Christopher's stepmom would be uncomplicated. There were no apparent transition issues when his dad and I got married. There were no custody issues since he spent half his time with his mom and the other half with us.

We fell into an easy going rhythm.

Until shit hit the fan.

Richard and I had been married four months when we went out for a few hours one Saturday morning. We had Christopher for the weekend and we told him where we were going and when we'd be back. We invited him to come along, but he said he wanted to stay home.

When Richard and I returned, I noticed what looked like brownie mix splatter on the door to the pantry. I didn't think much of it until I saw the same dark brown spots on the office entry way molding and the office walls. I looked closer. They were knife marks in my walls!

When we confronted Christopher, he lied. He swore that he had no idea how those knife marks appeared. Richard desperately wanted to believe his son but the evidence said otherwise.

A few weekends later, I offered to take Christopher even though my husband was working and it wasn't his weekend. I had no reason to believe anything was wrong but when I woke up on Saturday morning, I discovered that someone had taken a serrated blade to my suede couch and slashed a "Z" in the middle cushion.

"Did you do this?" I yelled as I pointed to the slash marks.

He looked at his feet and shook his head.

"Who did then?" I seethed. "You and I are the only ones in the house."

I noticed a steak knife on my coffee table and picked it up. "Think twice before you answer," I said as I gave him my best death stare.

"Edgar did it," Christopher replied. His face twitched. He looked like he had just stepped in a pile of poo.

"Edgar is a dog," I hissed. "He doesn't have opposable thumbs."

I shook with anger. All I wanted to do was pack up my stepson and drive him to his mother's. I didn't want him living in my home and I most certainly didn't want to be his stepmother.

My husband and his ex-wife made an appointment with Christopher's neurologist. They thought it was ADHD related. I believed it was anger, not ADHD, and this was how Christopher chose to express it. Christopher's neurologist offered no help except to tell him that ADHD wasn't an excuse to destroy property.

Christopher's mom emailed me the next day, to ask if it would be okay to have him stay with us that night. I took a deep breath and typed, "He can't stay here until he's in therapy."

You'd have thought I launched a nuclear bomb. Christopher's mom called my husband screaming at him that I had no business making a unilateral decision concerning their son.

Richard called and chewed me out. Who was I to make that decision by myself?

We were all right and we were all wrong.

Richard and I both left work early and when we got home, we had our first excruciatingly painful argument. He knew he was wrong for taking his ex-wife's side before he heard me out. I knew I was wrong for hitting the send key without discussing it with Richard first...and to be honest, this was his call, not mine. Christopher's mom was wrong because she knew something deeper was going on with her son yet she remained silent.

Richard was right because I didn't talk to him first. His ex-wife was right because it wasn't my decision to make. I was right because this issue with Christopher needed to be out in the open, talked about, and corrective action taken.

My husband found a therapist for Christopher and the three of us attended twice weekly counseling appointments. At the end of eight weeks, we were no closer to an answer for Christopher, but my husband and I were on the same page when it came to his son.

Before he began 10th grade, not only did I welcome Chris back into our home, but he came to live with us full time. As a reconstituted family we had our challenges. However, Richard and I were now a solid united front. There was nothing Chris could do to cause chaos in our home. We found another counselor and spent the next 2 years doing everything we could to get Chris ready for life after high school.

One particular session helped me reframe my perspective. I desperately wanted Chris to feel confident and successful, but nothing I did worked against 14 years of learned behavior. Christopher's counselor sensed my frustration and spoke these magic words:

"You did not break him. You cannot change him. And it's not your job to fix him. Your only job," he paused, *"is to love him."*

Holy freaking moly! The skies parted and angels sang. The pressure I felt to fix him dissolved. To this day I choose to love

Christopher, a child I never gave birth to, but who instead, was the gift my husband gave me when we said, "I do."

***

Christopher pushed open the door to the recovery room. "Thank you for being here," he whispered. He led me to the bassinet where his new baby daughter was stretched out under the heat lamp. I touched her feet and her delicate hands. I gazed upon the most perfect little baby and placed my hand on her warm pink chest.

"Hello Claire," I whispered as I picked her up. "I'm your GiGi."

ABOUT THE AUTHOR

Peggy Nolan is the co-author of four bestselling books and the host of the wildly popular podcast, Let Go Move Forward. Her work has appeared in Huffington Post, Aspire Magazine, and StepMom Magazine. This is her first book of poetry. Peggy lives in Derry, New Hampshire with her husband, Richard.

You can connect with Peggy at www.peggynolan.com.

www.ingramcontent.com/pod-product-compliance
Lightning Source LLC
Chambersburg PA
CBHW071738020426
42331CB00008B/2084